QUILTING IN
Black & White

Created for Leisure Arts by House of White Birches

QUILTING IN
Black & White

LEISURE ARTS STAFF

Editor-in-Chief **Susan White Sullivan**
Quilt Publications Director **Cheryl Johnson**
Special Projects Director **Susan Frantz Wiles**
Senior Prepress Director **Mark Hawkins**
Art Publications Director **Rhonda Shelby**
Imaging Technician **Stephanie Johnson**
Prepress Technician **Janie Marie Wright**
Publishing Systems Administrator **Becky Riddle**
Mac Information Technology Specialist **Robert Young**

President and Chief Executive Officer **Rick Barton**
Vice President and Chief Operations Officer **Tom Siebenmorgen**
Vice President of Sales **Mike Behar**
Director of Finance and Administration **Laticia Mull Dittrich**
National Sales Director **Martha Adams**
Creative Services **Chaska Lucas**
Information Technology Director **Hermine Linz**
Controller **Francis Caple**
Vice President, Operations **Jim Dittrich**
Retail Customer Service Manager **Stan Raynor**
Print Production Manager **Fred F. Pruss**

HOUSE OF WHITE BIRCHES STAFF

Editor **Jeanne Stauffer**
Art Director **Brad Snow**
Publishing Services Director **Brenda Gallmeyer**
Editorial Assistant **Stephanie Franklin**
Assistant Art Director **Nick Pierce**
Copy Supervisor **Deborah Morgan**
Copy Editors **Emily Carter, Mary O'Donnell**
Technical Editor **Sandra L. Hatch**
Technical Proofreader **Angie Buckles**
Production Artist Supervisor **Erin Augsburger**
Graphic Artist **Amanda Treharn**
Production Assistants **Marj Morgan, Judy Neuenschwander**
Technical Artist **Debera Kuntz**
Photography Supervisor **Tammy Christian**
Photography **Scott Campbell, Matthew Owen**
Photo Stylists **Tammy Liechty, Tammy Steiner**

Library of Congress Control Number: 2011927785
ISBN-13/EAN: 978-1-60900-358-6

10 9 8 7 6 5 4 3 2 1

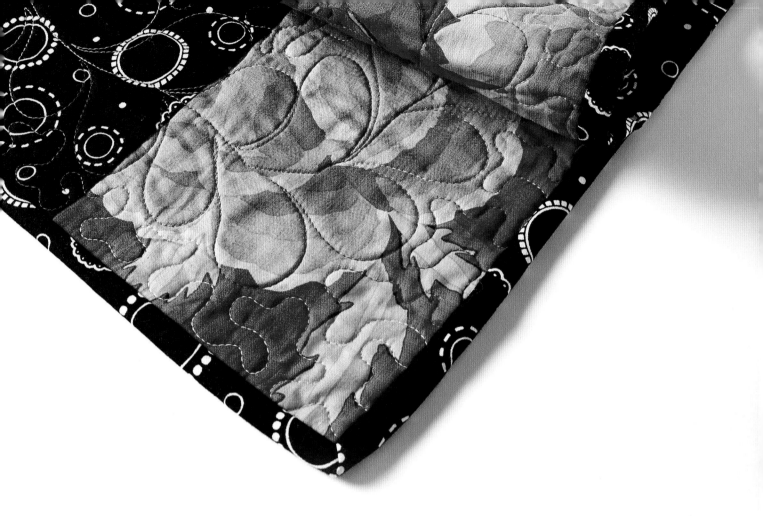

Introduction

Explore the world of quilting in black and white.

Quilts usually have color and lots of it. However, if you add a little or a lot of black and white to your quilt pattern, you will add more than a little drama to your project, and you'll end up with a quilt that is both striking and unique. It all starts with black and white fabrics.

When you collect the fabrics for your quilt, you will gradually realize that both white fabrics and black fabrics can be divided into lights, mediums and darks, the same as any other color of fabric. If you want to start experimenting with black and white fabrics in a small way, stitch the seven hot pads featured at the beginning of the book: Some are totally black and white, several have a little added color and a couple of them have bright color added with black used as a background to the brights.

The quilt patterns at the front of the book use only black and white fabrics. From the playful kitten wall quilt and the crazy quilt throw, you can see that both contemporary and traditional designs can be stitched with totally black and white fabrics. As you progress through the book, you will see more and more color added to the quilts. Some quilts demand bits of color, like the red cardinals in the White Birches design on page 31. In Children's Silhouette on page 50, the yellow and black fabrics outline and serve as a background for the panels. The last project in the book, titled In the Pink, explodes with color across the quilt with black and white fabric adding drama and creating a counterpoint to the eye-catching pink prints.

If you haven't tried quilting with black and white fabrics, now is the time to start. When you make the quilts in this book, you'll learn for yourself the beauty to be found in black and white.

TABLE OF Contents

Cat at Play, 15

White Birches, 31

Night & Day, 21

Starry Lane, 55

Black & White Plus Red, 45

In the Pink, 59

Sophisticated Crazy Patch, 25

My Rose of Sharon, 38

Children's Silhouette, 50

Dramatic Impact

DESIGNS BY TRICE BOERENS

The addition of black fabric to the colors of these hot pads inspired their theatrical names.

Project Specifications

Skill Level: Beginner
Finished Size: 8" x 8"

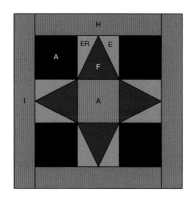

Gypsy Lee
Placement Diagram
8" x 8"

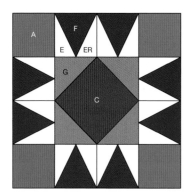

Stagestruck
Placement Diagram
8" x 8"

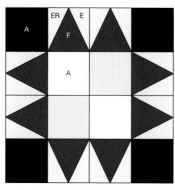

Bright Lights
Placement Diagram
8" x 8"

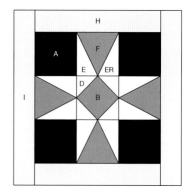

Opening Night
Placement Diagram
8" x 8"

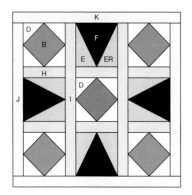

Repertory Group
Placement Diagram
8" x 8"

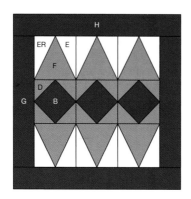

Walk of Fame
Placement Diagram
8" x 8"

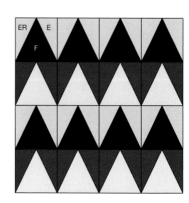

Highs & Lows
Placement Diagram
8" x 8"

Project Notes

These projects are made from scraps using templates (pages 8, 10 and 11) to cut each piece. Be sure to match the grain-line marks on the templates to the grain-line of the scrap piece you are using.

It is advised that you use heat-resistant materials to make the hot pads. Use 100 percent cotton fabrics and threads. Use three layers of cotton or special heat-resistant batting (like Insul-Bright) to achieve the best protection from heat.

All hot pads are the same size and skill level. Each hot-pad pattern contains a piecing diagram that shows assembly ideas.

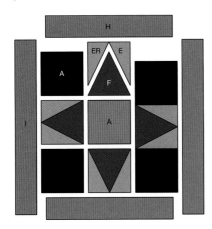

Piecing Diagram

Gypsy Lee

Materials

- Assorted fabric scraps at least 3" square in black print, black floral, white dot and large rose floral
- 1 fat quarter rose tonal
- 1 fat quarter burgundy print
- 3 (10" x 10") squares heat-resistant batting
- Backing 10" x 10"
- Neutral-color all-purpose cotton thread
- Quilting thread
- 1 (1") plastic ring (optional)
- 1 (8" x 10") sheet template material
- Fine-tip permanent marker
- Chalk or lead pencil
- Fabric basting spray (optional)
- Basic sewing tools and supplies

Cutting

1. Place the template material over A, E, ER and F templates and trace the shapes using a fine-tip permanent marker. Transfer the grain-line arrows and add name labels to each template. Cut templates out on the traced line.

2. Place the prepared template right side down on the wrong side of indicated fabric matching fabric grain to marked grain line.

3. Referring to steps 4-6 for number to trace and cut, trace around the template shape with a chalk or lead pencil. Cut out shapes on marked lines.

4. Fussy-cut one A from the large rose floral scrap and four A pieces from the black print scraps.

5. Cut four each E and ER from white dot scraps.

6. Cut four F from the black floral scraps.

7. From the rose tonal fat quarter, cut two 1½" x 6½" H strips and two 1½" x 8½" I strips.

8. From the burgundy print fat quarter, cut two 2" x 22" strips for binding.

Completing the Hot Pad

1. Sew E and ER to F to make a side unit referring to the piecing diagram. Press seams away from F. Repeat to make four side units.

2. Sew a side unit to opposite sides of the floral A to make the center row. Press seams toward A.

3. Sew a black print A to each side of a side unit to make a side row. Press seams away from the side unit. Repeat to make two side rows.

4. Sew the center row between the side rows; press seams away from the center row.

5. Sew H to the top and bottom, and I to opposite sides of the pieced center; press seams toward H and I to complete the pieced top.

6. Layer, quilt and bind referring to Finishing Your Quilt on page 64 to complete the hot pad.

7. If desired, hand-sew the 1" plastic ring to one corner of the completed hot pad for hanging.

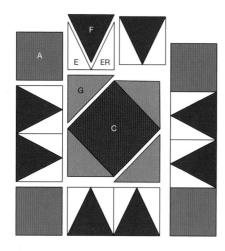

Piecing Diagram

Stagestruck

Materials

- Assorted fabric scraps at least 4" square in magenta mottled, purple tonal, black floral and black print
- 1 fat quarter white solid
- 1 fat quarter purple print
- 3 (10" x 10") squares heat-resistant batting
- Backing 10" x 10"
- Neutral-color all-purpose cotton thread
- Quilting thread
- 1 (1") plastic ring (optional)
- 1 (8" x 10") sheet template material
- Fine-tip permanent marker
- Chalk or lead pencil
- Fabric basting spray (optional)
- Basic sewing tools and supplies

Cutting

1. Place the template material over A, C, E, ER, F and G templates and trace the shapes using a fine-tip permanent marker. Transfer the grain-line arrows and add name labels to each template. Cut templates out on the traced line.

2. Place the prepared template right side down on the wrong side of indicated fabric matching fabric grain to marked grain line.

3. Referring to steps 4-8 for number to trace and cut, trace around the template shape with a chalk or lead pencil. Cut out shapes on marked lines.

4. Cut one C from the magenta mottled scrap.

5. Cut four A pieces from the purple tonal scraps.

6. Cut eight F pieces from the black floral scraps.

7. Cut four G pieces from the black print scraps.

8. From the white solid fat quarter, cut eight each E and ER pieces.

9. From the purple print fat quarter, cut two 2" x 22" strips for binding.

Completing the Hot Pad

1. Sew G to each side of C to complete the center unit. Press seams toward G.

2. Sew E and ER to F to complete a triangle unit; press seams away from F. Repeat to make eight triangle units.

3. Join two triangle units together to make a side unit; press seam in one direction. Repeat to make four side units.

4. Sew a side unit to opposite sides of the center unit to complete the center row; press seams toward the center unit.

5. Sew A to each end of each remaining side unit to make side rows. Press seams toward A.

6. Sew the side rows to opposite sides of the center row to complete the pieced top. Press seams toward the side rows.

7. Layer, quilt and bind referring to Finishing Your Quilt on page 64 to complete the hot pad.

8. If desired, hand-sew the 1" plastic ring to one corner of the completed hot pad for hanging.

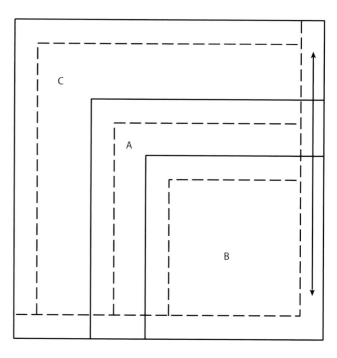

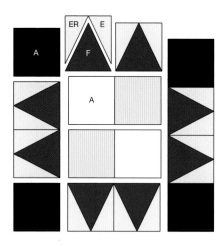

Piecing Diagram

Bright Lights

Materials

- Assorted fabric scraps at least 4" square in white solid, peach mottled, black solid and black print
- 1 fat quarter cream tonal
- 1 fat quarter rust mottled
- 3 (10" x 10") squares heat-resistant batting
- Backing 10" x 10"
- Neutral-color all-purpose cotton thread
- Quilting thread
- 1 (1") plastic ring (optional)
- 1 (8" x 10") sheet template material
- Fine-tip permanent marker
- Chalk or lead pencil
- Fabric basting spray (optional)
- Basic sewing tools and supplies

Cutting

1. Place the template material over A, E, ER and F templates and trace the shapes using a fine-tip permanent marker. Transfer the grain-line arrows and add name labels to each template. Cut templates out on the traced line.

2. Place the prepared template right side down on the wrong side of indicated fabric matching fabric grain to marked grain-line.

3. Referring to steps 4-7 for number to trace and cut, trace around the template shape with a chalk or lead pencil. Cut out shapes on marked lines.

4. Cut two A pieces from each white solid and peach mottled scraps.

5. Cut four A pieces from the black solid scraps.

6. Cut eight F pieces from the black print scraps.

7. From the cream tonal fat quarter, cut eight each of the E and ER pieces.

8. From the rust mottled fat quarter, cut two 2" x 22" strips for binding.

Completing the Hot Pad

1. Sew a white A to a peach A; press seam toward darker fabric. Repeat to make two A rows.

2. Join the A rows to complete the center unit. Press seam in one direction.

3. Sew E and ER to long sides of F to complete a triangle unit. Press seams away from F. Repeat to make eight triangle units.

4. Join two triangle units to complete a side unit. Press seam in one direction. Repeat to make four side units.

5. Sew a side unit to opposite sides of the center unit to complete the center row. Press seams toward the center unit.

6. Sew a black solid A to each end of each remaining side unit to make side rows; press seams toward A.

7. Sew the side rows to opposite sides of the center row to complete the pieced top. Press seams toward the side rows.

8. Layer, quilt and bind referring to Finishing Your Quilt on page 64 to complete the hot pad.

9. If desired, hand-sew the 1" plastic ring to one corner of the completed hot pad for hanging.

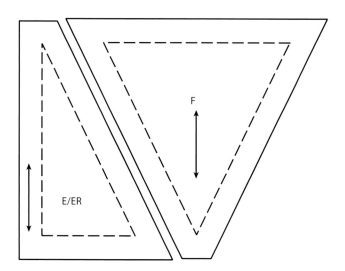

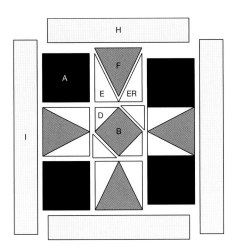

Piecing Diagram

Opening Night

Materials

- Assorted fabric scraps at least 3" square in white dot and black print
- 1 fat quarter yellow print
- 1 fat quarter black dot
- 1 fat quarter rust mottled
- 3 (10" x 10") squares heat-resistant batting
- Backing 10" x 10"
- Neutral-color all-purpose cotton thread
- Quilting thread
- 1 (1") plastic ring (optional)
- 1 (8" x 10") sheet template material
- Fine-tip permanent marker
- Chalk or lead pencil
- Fabric basting spray (optional)
- Basic sewing tools and supplies

Cutting

1. Place the template material over A, B, D, E, ER and F templates and trace the shapes using a fine-tip permanent marker. Transfer the grain-line arrows and add name labels to each template. Cut templates out on the traced line.

2. Place the prepared template right side down on the wrong side of indicated fabric matching fabric grain to marked grain line.

3. Referring to steps 4-7 for number to trace and cut, trace around the template shape with a chalk or lead pencil. Cut out shapes on marked lines.

4. Cut four A pieces from the black print scraps.

5. Cut four D pieces and four each E and ER pieces from the white dot scraps.

6. From the yellow print fat quarter, cut two 1½" x 6½" H strips and two 1½" x 8½" I strips.

7. From the black dot fat quarter, cut one B piece and four F pieces.

8. From the rust mottled fat quarter, cut two 2" x 22" strips for binding.

Completing the Hot Pad

1. Sew D to each side of B to complete the center unit; press seams toward D.

2. Sew E and ER to F to complete a side unit; press seams away from F. Repeat to make four side units.

3. Sew a side unit to opposite sides of the center unit to complete the center row; press seams toward the center unit.

4. Sew A to opposite sides of each remaining side unit to make side rows; press seams toward A.

5. Sew a side row to opposite sides of the center row; press seams toward side rows.

6. Sew H to the top and bottom, and I to opposite sides of the pieced rows to complete the pieced top. Press seams toward H and I.

7. Layer, quilt and bind referring to Finishing Your Quilt on page 64 to complete the hot pad.

8. If desired, hand-sew the 1" plastic ring to one corner of the completed hot pad for hanging.

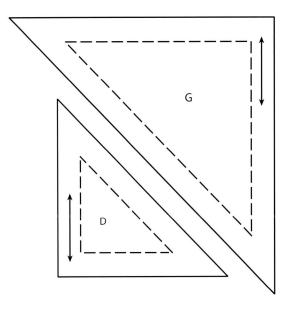

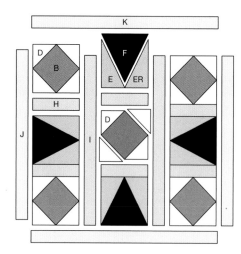

Piecing Diagram

Repertory Group

Materials

- Assorted fabric scraps at least 3" square in white dot, black dot and gray mottled
- 1 fat quarter cream tonal
- 1 fat quarter gray print
- 1 fat quarter black solid
- 3 (10" x 10") squares heat-resistant batting
- Backing 10" x 10"
- Neutral-color all-purpose cotton thread
- Quilting thread
- 1 (1") plastic ring (optional)
- 1 (8" x 10") sheet template material
- Fine-tip permanent marker
- Chalk or lead pencil
- Fabric basting spray (optional)
- Basic sewing tools and supplies

Cutting

1. Place the template material over B, D, E, ER and F templates and trace the shapes using a fine-tip permanent marker. Transfer the grain-line arrows and add name labels to each template. Cut templates out on the traced line.

2. Place the prepared template right side down on the wrong side of indicated fabric matching fabric grain to marked grain line.

3. Referring to steps 4–6 and 9 for number to trace and cut, trace around the template shape with a chalk or lead pencil. Cut out shapes on marked lines.

4. Cut five B pieces from the black dot scraps.

5. Cut 20 D pieces from the white dot scraps.

6. Cut four each E and ER from the gray mottled scraps.

7. From the cream tonal fat quarter, cut two 1" x 7½" J strips and two 1" x 8½" K strips.

8. From the gray print fat quarter, cut six 1" x 2½" H strips and two 1" x 7½" I strips.

9. From the black solid fat quarter, cut four F pieces and two 2" x 22" strips for binding.

Completing the Hot Pad

1. Sew D to each side of B to complete a B unit; press seams toward D. Repeat to make five B units.

2. Sew E and ER to F to complete a triangle unit; press seams away from F. Repeat to make four triangle units.

3. Join one triangle unit, two B units and two H strips to complete a side row; press seams toward H. Repeat to make two side rows.

4. Join one B unit with two triangle units and two H strips to complete the center row; press seams toward H.

5. Join the side and center rows with I to complete the pieced center; press seams toward I.

6. Sew J to opposite sides and K to the top and bottom of the pieced center to complete the pieced block. Press seams toward J and K.

7. Layer, quilt and bind referring to Finishing Your Quilt on page 64 to complete the hot pad.

8. If desired, hand-sew the 1" plastic ring to one corner of the completed hot pad for hanging.

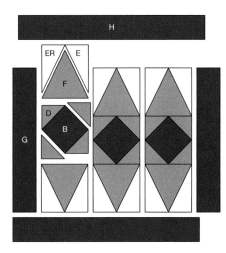

Piecing Diagram

Walk of Fame

Materials

- Assorted fabric scraps at least 3" square in black floral, black dot and white dot
- 1 fat quarter black floral
- 1 fat quarter wine solid
- 3 (10" x 10") squares heat-resistant batting
- Backing 10" x 10"
- Neutral-color all-purpose cotton thread
- Quilting thread
- 1 (1") plastic ring (optional)
- 1 (8" x 10") sheet template material
- Fine-tip permanent marker
- Chalk or lead pencil
- Fabric basting spray (optional)
- Basic sewing tools and supplies

Cutting

1. Place the template material over B, D, E, ER and F templates and trace the shapes using a fine-tip permanent marker. Transfer the grain-line arrows and add name labels to each template. Cut templates out on the traced line.

2. Place the prepared template right side down on the wrong side of indicated fabric matching fabric grain to marked grain line.

3. Referring to steps 4-6 for number to trace and cut, trace around the template shape with a chalk or lead pencil. Cut out shapes on marked lines.

4. Cut three B pieces from the black floral scraps.

5. Cut 12 D pieces and six F pieces from the black dot scraps.

6. Cut six each of E and ER from the white dot scraps.

7. From the black floral fat quarter, cut two 1½" x 6½" G strips and two 1½" x 8½" H strips.

8. From the wine solid fat quarter, cut two 2" x 22" strips for binding.

Completing the Hot Pad

1. Sew D to each side of B to complete a B unit; press seams toward D. Repeat to make three B units.

2. Sew E and ER to F to complete a triangle unit; press seams away from F. Repeat to make six triangle units.

3. Sew a triangle unit to opposite sides of a B unit to complete one row. Repeat to make three rows. Press seams of one row toward the triangle units and two rows toward the B unit.

4. Join the rows, alternating seam pressing, to complete the pieced center. Press seams in one direction.

5. Sew G to opposite sides and H to the top and bottom of the pieced center to complete the pieced top. Press seams toward H and G.

6. Layer, quilt and bind referring to Finishing Your Quilt on page 64 to complete the hot pad.

7. If desired, hand-sew the 1" plastic ring to one corner of the completed hot pad for hanging.

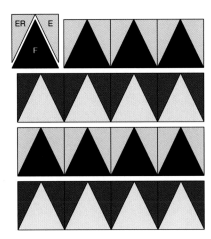

Piecing Diagram

Highs & Lows

Materials

- Assorted fabric scraps at least 3" square in gray mottled, black print, black solid and gray print
- ⅛ yard pink stripe
- 3 (10" x 10") squares heat-resistant batting
- Backing 10" x 10"
- Neutral-color all-purpose cotton thread
- Quilting thread
- 1 (1") plastic ring (optional)
- 1 (8" x 10") sheet template material
- Fine-tip permanent marker
- Chalk or lead pencil
- Fabric basting spray (optional)
- Basic sewing tools and supplies

Cutting

1. Place the template material over E, ER and F templates and trace the shapes using a fine-tip permanent marker. Transfer the grain-line arrows and add name labels to each template. Cut templates out on the traced line.

2. Place the prepared template right side down on the wrong side of indicated fabric matching fabric grain to marked grain line.

3. Referring to steps 4 and 5 for number to trace and cut, trace around the template shape with a chalk or lead pencil. Cut out shapes on marked lines.

4. Cut eight each E and ER from the gray mottled scraps and eight each E and ER from the black print scraps.

5. Cut eight F pieces from the black solid scraps and eight F pieces from gray print scraps.

6. From the pink stripe, cut one 1" x 36" strip for binding.

Completing the Hot Pad

1. Sew a black print E and ER to a gray print F to make a gray triangle unit. Press seams away from F. Repeat to make eight gray triangle units.

2. Join four gray triangle units to make a gray row; press seams in one direction. Repeat to make two gray rows.

3. Sew a gray mottled E and ER to a black F to make a black triangle unit. Press seams away from F. Repeat to make eight black triangle units.

4. Join four black triangle units to make a black row; press seams in one direction. Repeat to make two black rows.

5. Arrange and join the rows referring to the Piecing Diagram to complete the pieced top. Press seams in one direction.

6. Layer, quilt and bind referring to Finishing Your Quilt on page 64 to complete the hot pad.

7. If desired, hand-sew the 1" plastic ring to one corner of the completed hot pad for hanging. ❑

Cat at Play

DESIGN BY NANCY VASILCHIK

A playful wall quilt with a cat design is striking stitched in black-and-white prints.

Project Specifications

Skill Level: Intermediate
Quilt Size: 34" x 26"

Materials

- ⅛ yard each 6 black-with-white prints or dots
- ⅛ yard each 6 white-with-black prints
- ⅜ yard black-with-white print for N/O borders

- ½ yard white-with-black message print
- ¾ yard black solid
- Backing 40" x 32"
- Batting 40" x 32"
- Black all-purpose thread
- Quilting thread
- ½ yard fusible web
- Basic sewing tools and supplies

Cutting

1. Cut one 18½" x 10½" A rectangle white-with-black message print.

2. Cut one 2½" black-with-white prints or dots strip in each of the following sizes: 18½" B, 14½" D, 22½" F, 22½" G, 18½" H and 18½" I.

3. Cut one 2½" white-with-black prints strip in each of the following sizes: 18½" C, 14½" E, 26½" J, 26½" K, 22½" L and 22½" M.

4. Cut two 2½" x 30½" N strips and two 2½" x 26½" O strips black-with-white print.

5. Cut two 1" x 8" strips each two different white-with-black prints and three 1" x 8" strips each three different black-with-white prints or dots for strip-pieced section for yarn applique pieces.

6. Cut four 2¼" by fabric width strips black solid for binding.

7. Trace the cat and cat tail shapes (page 19) onto the paper side of the fusible web; cut out shapes, leaving a margin all around.

8. Fuse the shapes to the wrong side of the fabrics as directed on patterns for color; cut out shapes on traced lines. Remove paper backing.

9. Prepare templates for yarn sections using patterns given (page 18); mark seam lines on templates for sections 1–3 as indicated on patterns. Cut section 4 piece as directed.

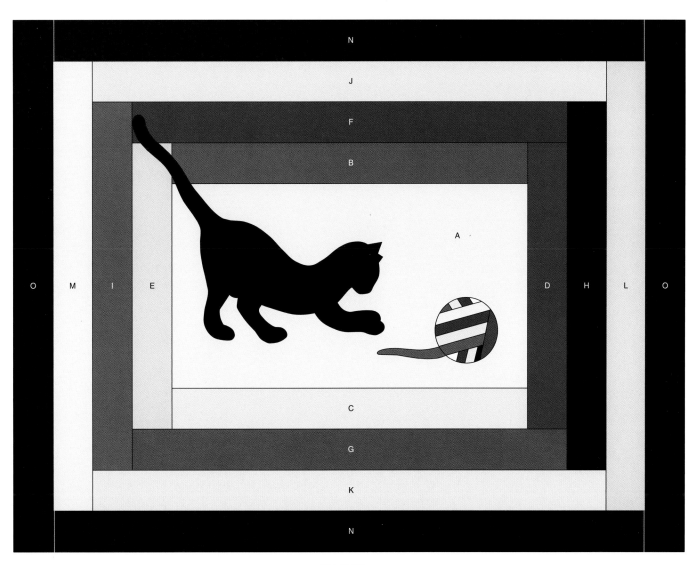

Cat at Play
Placement Diagram 34" x 26"

Completing the Quilt

1. Sew the 2½"-wide strips (B–O) to A in alphabetical order referring to the Placement Diagram, pressing seams toward strips before adding another strip.

2. Sew the 1"-wide strips together, alternating colors, to make a strip-pieced section as shown in Figure 1.

Figure 1

3. Trace template sections onto the pieced section as shown in Figure 2; cut out shapes, including seam allowances as marked on templates.

Figure 2

4. Join the sections to complete the strip-pieced yarn ball as shown in Figure 3.

Figure 3

5. Mark a 3¼" circle onto the paper side of the fusible web; cut out on traced lines. Center and fuse to the wrong side of the strip-pieced yarn ball; remove paper backing.

6. Place and pin the cat shape and ball on the pieced background referring to the Placement Diagram for positioning; tuck the yarn tail piece under the ball at the matching-fabric end as shown in Figure 4. Fuse all pieces in place.

Figure 4

7. Using a blind hemstitch and black thread, stitch all around edges of appliqué shapes to finish.

8. Layer, quilt and bind referring to Finishing Your Quilt on page 64. □

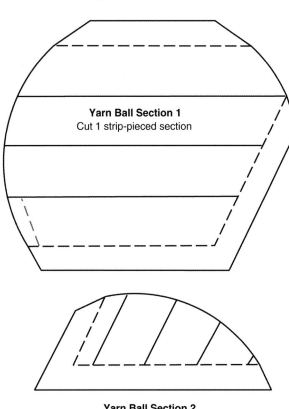

Yarn Ball Section 1
Cut 1 strip-pieced section

Yarn Ball Section 2
Cut 1 strip-pieced section

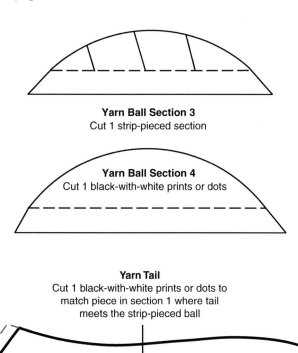

Yarn Ball Section 3
Cut 1 strip-pieced section

Yarn Ball Section 4
Cut 1 black-with-white prints or dots

Yarn Tail
Cut 1 black-with-white prints or dots to match piece in section 1 where tail meets the strip-pieced ball

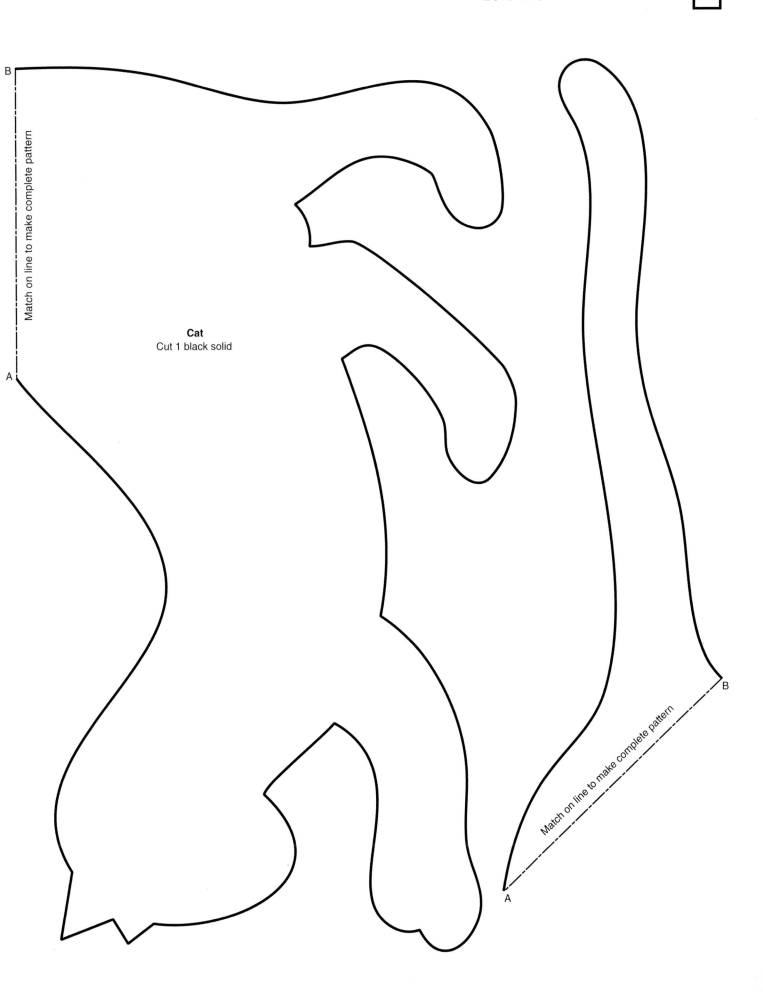

B

Match on line to make complete pattern

A

Cat
Cut 1 black solid

B

Match on line to make complete pattern

A

Night & Day

DESIGN BY SANDRA L. HATCH

Using black and white prints makes a bold statement, showing off the Flying Geese circling at dusk.

Project Specifications

Quilt Size: 48" x 48"
Block Size: 12" x 12"
Number of Blocks: 4

Materials

- ¼ yard black solid
- ¾ yard each 3 different black-with-white prints
- ¾ yard black-and-white stripe
- 1⅞ yards white-with-black print
- Backing 52" x 52"
- Batting 52" x 52"
- Black and white all-purpose threads
- Black machine-quilting thread
- Basic sewing tools and supplies

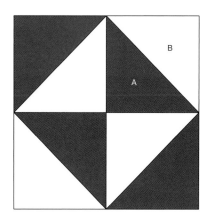

Broken Dishes
12" x 12" Block
Make 4

Cutting

1. Cut one 4½" by fabric width strip of black solid. Subcut four 4½" E squares.

2. Cut a total of eight 6⅞" squares from the three different black-with-white prints. Cut each square in half on one diagonal for a total of 16 A triangles.

3. Cut a total of 19 strips 2½" by fabric width from the black-with-white prints. Subcut strips into 304 (2½") D squares.

4. Cut a total of nine 4½" F squares from the black-with-white prints. **Note:** *For a less busy quilt, add ¼ yard to the black solid fabric amount and cut the F squares from the black solid.*

5. From the black-and-white stripe, cut two G strips 2½" x 36½" and two H strips 2½" x 40½".

6. Cut five 2¼" by fabric width strips black-and-white stripe for binding.

7. From the white-with-black print, cut two strips 6⅞" by fabric width. Subcut into eight 6⅞" squares. Cut each square on one diagonal to make a total of 16 B triangles.

8. Cut 10 strips 4½" by fabric width from the white-with-black print. Subcut into 152 (2½" x 4½") C rectangles.

Completing the Broken Dishes Blocks

1. Sew an A and B triangle together to make an A/B unit as shown in Figure 1. Repeat to make 16 A/B units.

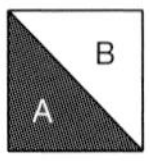

Figure 1

2. Join two A/B units as shown in Figure 2 to make eight A/B rows.

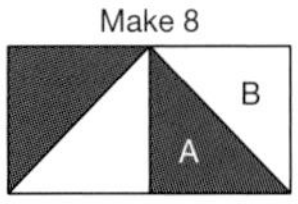

Make 8

Figure 2

3. Join two A/B rows to complete one Broken Dishes block referring to the block diagram. Repeat to make four blocks. Set aside.

Completing the Flying Geese Units

1. Draw a diagonal line from corner to corner on the wrong side of each D square.

2. Place a D square on one corner of a C rectangle and stitch on drawn line as shown in Figure 3.

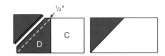

Figure 3

3. Trim seam to ¼" and press D to the right side, again referring to Figure 3.

4. Repeat on the opposite end of C to complete a C/D Flying Geese unit as shown in Figure 4; repeat to make 152 Flying Geese units. Set aside.

Figure 4

Completing the Quilt

1. Join three Flying Geese units, as shown in Figure 5, to make a triple Flying Geese unit. Press seams in one direction.

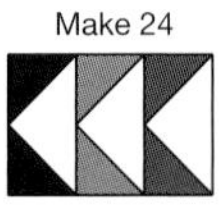

Make 24

Figure 5

2. Repeat to make 24 triple Flying Geese units.

3. Join two triple Flying Geese units to make a Flying Geese sashing strip with the geese flying in opposite directions as shown in Figure 6.

Make 12

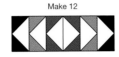

Figure 6

4. Repeat to make 12 sashing strips.

5. Join two Broken Dishes blocks with three Flying Geese sashing strips as shown in Figure 7 to make a block row. Press seams toward blocks.

Make 2

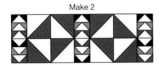

Figure 7

6. Repeat to make two block rows.

7. Join two Flying Geese sashing strips with three F squares to make a sashing row as shown in Figure 8. Press seams toward D.

Make 3

Figure 8

8. Repeat to make three sashing rows.

9. Join the block rows with the sashing rows referring to the Placement Diagram to complete the quilt pieced center. Press seams toward block rows.

10. Sew G strips to the top and bottom, and H strips to opposite sides of the pieced center. Press seams toward strips.

11. Join 20 Flying Geese units to make a border strip as shown in Figure 9. Press seams in one direction.

Make 4

Figure 9

12. Repeat to make four Flying Geese border strips.

13. Sew a border strip to opposite sides of the pieced center, referring to the Placement Diagram. Press seams away from border strips.

14. Sew an E square to each end of the remaining two border strips. Sew to the remaining sides of the pieced center, referring to the Placement Diagram. Press seams away from the border strips.

15. Layer, quilt and bind referring to Finishing Your Quilt on page 64. ◻

Night & Day
Placement Diagram
48" x 48"

Sophisticated Crazy Patch

DESIGN BY NANCY VASILCHIK

You can still have symmetry and order in a crazy quilt.

Project Specifications

Skill Level: Beginner
Quilt Size: 48" x 69"
Block Size: 13" x 15"
Number of Blocks: 12

Materials

- 6 fat quarters black-with-white prints
- 6 fat quarters white-with-black prints
- ¾ yard black-and-white print
- ⅞ yard white solid
- 1⅝ yards bleached muslin
- 1⅞ yards black solid
- Batting 54" x 75"
- Backing 54" x 75"
- All-purpose thread to match fabrics
- Black and white decorative threads
- Quilting thread
- 2⅓ yards lightweight tear-off fabric stabilizer
- Water-erasable marker or chalk pencil
- Basic sewing tools and supplies

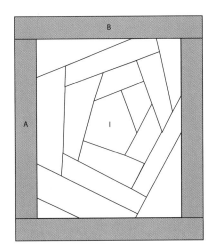

White/Black Crazy
13" x 15" Block
Make 6

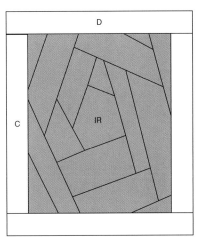

Black/White Crazy
13" x 15" Block
Make 6

Cutting

1. Prepare template for I/IR using pattern given (page 29); transfer centering lines to template.

2. Stack the white-with-black fat quarters right side up to make a white set.

3. Place the template on the white set and cut as shown in Figure 1; cut the remainder of the stack into strips as marked in Figure 1, starting cutting with the first measurement and increasing or decreasing size to the opposite side as indicated in Figure 1. Transfer the positioning lines to the I pieces using a water-erasable marker or chalk pencil.

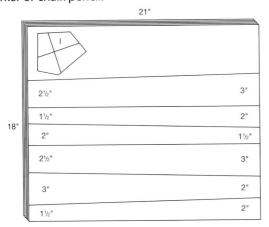

Figure 1

4. Repeat steps 2 and 3 with the black-with-white fat quarters, reversing the I/IR template as shown in Figure 2.

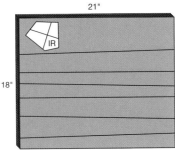

Figure 2

5. Cut two 2" x 60½" E strips along the length of the black solid.

6. Cut two 2" x 42½" F strips along the length of the black solid.

7. Cut one 12½" by remaining fabric width strip black solid; subcut strip into 12 (2") A strips.

8. Cut one 13½" by remaining fabric width strip black solid; subcut strip into 12 (2") B strips.

9. Cut eight 2¼" by remaining fabric width strips black solid for binding.

10. Cut one 12½" by fabric width strip white solid; subcut strip into 12 (2") C strips.

11. Cut one 13½" by fabric width strip white solid; subcut strip into 12 (2") D strips.

12. Cut six 3½" by fabric width G/H strips black-and-white print.

13. Cut four 13" by fabric width strips bleached muslin; subcut strips into 12 (11") muslin base rectangles.

Completing the Blocks

1. Draw a horizontal and vertical line through the center of each muslin base as shown in Figure 3.

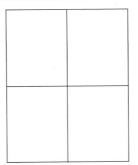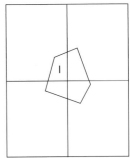

Figure 3   **Figure 4**

2. To complete one white/black unit, pin one white-with-black I piece on a muslin base, matching the lines on the muslin with the lines on I as shown in Figure 4.

3. Using all white-with-black strips, select one strip; place it right sides together with the pinned I piece, extending strip beyond the I piece at the beginning and end as shown in Figure 5.

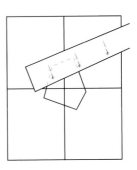

Figure 5

4. Stitch using a ¼" seam. Trim the strip to extend slightly beyond the edge of I; press the strip to the right side as shown in Figure 6.

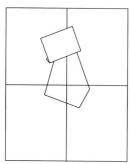

Figure 6

5. Continue adding strips clockwise around the sides of I until all sides of I are covered as shown in Figure 7.

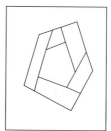

Figure 7

6. Continue adding strips around the center in this manner until the muslin base is covered. ***Note:*** *Outer pieces will extend past the muslin.*

7. Turn the completed piece over and trim excess even with the muslin base.

8. Repeat steps 2–7 to complete six white/black units.

9. Repeat steps 2–7 with black-with-white fabrics to complete six black/white units referring to the block drawing.

10. Cut 12 (11" x 13") rectangles lightweight, tear-off fabric stabilizer.

11. Pin a piece of stabilizer to the wrong side of each unit.

12. Using black decorative thread on the white/black units and white decorative thread on the black/white units, add a decorative machine stitch on each seam.

13. After decorative stitching is complete, trim each unit to 10½" x 12½". Remove fabric stabilizer.

14. Sew an A strip to opposite sides and B strips to the top and bottom of each white/black unit to complete the White/Black blocks; press seams toward A and B strips.

15. Sew a C strip to opposite sides and D strips to the top and bottom of each black/white unit to complete the Black/White blocks; press seams toward C and D strips.

Completing the Top

1. Sew a Black/White block between two White/Black blocks to make an X row; press seams toward the White/Black blocks. Repeat to make two X rows.

2. Sew a White/Black block between two Black/White blocks to make a Y row; press seams toward White/Black block. Repeat to make two Y rows.

3. Join the X and Y rows referring to the Placement Diagram to complete the pieced center; press seams in one direction.

4. Sew an E strip to opposite long sides and F strips to the top and bottom of the pieced center; press seams toward E and F strips.

5. Join the G/H strips on short ends to make one long strip; subcut strip into two 63½" G strips and two 48½" H strips.

6. Sew a G strip to opposite long sides and H strips to the top and bottom of the pieced center; press seams toward G and H strips to complete the pieced top.

7. Layer, quilt and bind referring to Finishing Your Quilt on page 64. □

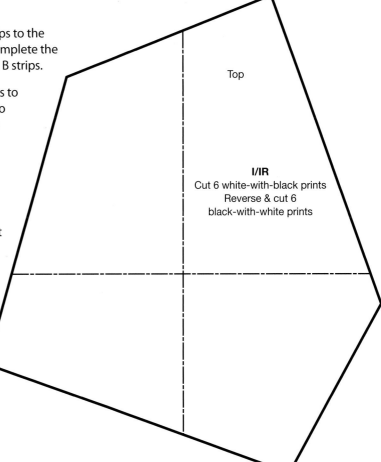

Top

I/IR
Cut 6 white-with-black prints
Reverse & cut 6
black-with-white prints

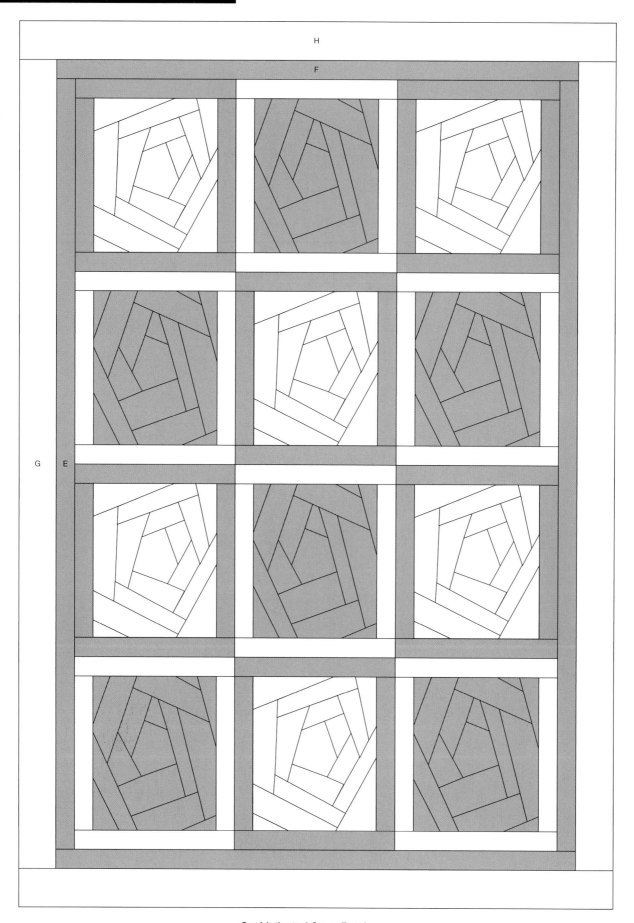

Sophisticated Crazy Patch
Placement Diagram 48" x 69"

White Birches

DESIGN BY GINA GEMPESAW, QUILTED BY CAROLE WHALING

Sometimes we can't see the forest for the trees. Removing the leaves reveals a simple but graphic architecture.

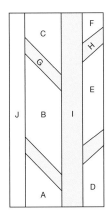

White Birch
9" x 18" Block
Make 3 light,
3 medium & 2 dark

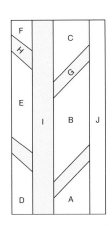

Reverse White Birch
9" x 18" Block
Make 1 light, 1 medium
& 2 dark

Project Specifications

Skill Level: Advanced
Quilt Size: 53" x 71"
Block Size: 9" x 18"
Number of Blocks: 12

Materials

- Scraps gold tonals and black solid
- ⅜ yard red tonal
- ⅜ yard dark black-and-white print
- ⅜ yard medium black-and-white print
- ⅜ yard light black-and-white print
- ⅝ yard gray mottled
- ⅝ yard black print
- 3½ yards white tonal
- Backing 61" x 79"
- Batting 61" x 79"
- All-purpose thread to match fabrics
- ¼ yard 18"-wide fusible web
- Ruler with 45-degree angle line
- Basic sewing tools and supplies

Cutting

1. Cut six 1½" x fabric width strips from the red tonal for O/P.

2. From the dark black-and-white print, cut three 1⅝" by fabric width strips. Subcut into eight 1⅝" x 8" G rectangles and eight 1⅝" x 6" H rectangles.

3. Cut two 2¼" by fabric width strips from the dark black-and-white print. Subcut four 2¼" x 18½" I strips.

4. From the medium black-and-white print, cut three 1⅝" by fabric width strips. Subcut into eight 1⅝" x 8" G rectangles and eight 1⅝" x 6" H rectangles.

5. Cut two 2¼" by fabric width strips from the medium black-and-white print. Subcut four 2¼" x 18½" I strips.

6. From the light black-and-white print, cut three 1⅝" by fabric width strips. Subcut into eight 1⅝" x 8" G rectangles and eight 1⅝" x 6" H rectangles.

7. Cut two 2¼" by fabric width strips from the light black-and-white print. Subcut four 2¼" x 18½" I strips.

8. From the gray mottled, cut six 2½" x fabric width strips for M/N.

9. From the black print, cut seven 2¼" x fabric width strips for binding.

10. From the white tonal, cut three 18½" by fabric width strips. Subcut into 12 (4½" x 18½") A/B/C rectangles and 12 (2¾" x 18½") D/E/F rectangles and 12 (2" x 18½") J strips.

11. Along length of white tonal, cut two 3½" x 54½" K borders, two 3½" x 42½" L borders, two 4" x 64½" Q borders, two 4" x 46½" R borders and four 4" x 4½" S rectangles.

Completing the Blocks

1. Lay a 4½" x 18½" A/B/C rectangle right side up on a flat surface; measure up 6" from the bottom left corner and mark; measure up and mark 8½" from the first mark referring to Figure 1.

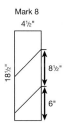

Figure 1

2. Cut the rectangle from edge to edge at a 45-degree angle to make pieces A, B and C as shown in Figure 2.

Figure 2

3. Pin these three cut pieces together as a set. Repeat with seven more rectangles to make a total of eight A, B, C sets.

4. Lay a 2¾" x 18½" D/E/F rectangle right side up on a flat surface. Measure 6¾" from the bottom right corner and mark; measure up and mark 8½" from the first mark referring to Figure 3.

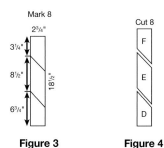

Figure 3   **Figure 4**

5. Repeat step 2 to make pieces D, E and F as shown in Figure 4.

6. Pin these three cut pieces together as a set. Repeat with seven more rectangles to make a total of eight D, E, F sets.

7. Repeat steps 1–6, marking on the right edges to create four reverse A, B, C sets and on the left edges to make four reverse D, E, F sets as shown in Figure 5.

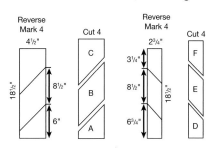

Figure 5

8. Select two each light G and light H strips.

9. Place a light G strip between pieces A, B and C, aligning edges of A, B and C as shown in Figure 6; stitch to join the segments. Press seams away from G.

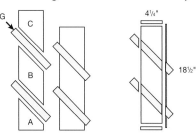

Figure 6   Figure 7

10. Trim the excess G even with the A, B and C pieces; trim the unit to 4¼" x 18½" to complete one light large branch unit as shown in Figure 7.

11. Repeat steps 9 and 10 with light H strips and a D, E, F set and trim to 2½" x 18½" as shown in Figure 8 to make a light small branch unit; press seams toward H strips.

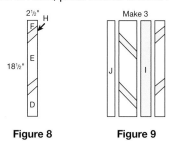

Figure 8   Figure 9

12. Join the two branch units with a light I and add J as shown in Figure 9 to complete one light White Birch block; press seams toward I and J strips.

13. Repeat steps 8–12 to make a total of three light White Birch blocks.

14. Repeat steps 8–12 with one each reverse A, B, C and D, E, F sets to make one light Reverse White Birch block as shown in Figure 10.

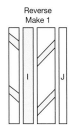

Reverse
Make 1

Figure 10

15. Repeat steps 8–12 with medium G, H and I strips to complete three medium White Birch blocks and one medium Reverse White Birch block as shown in Figure 11.

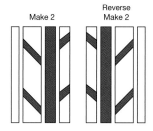

Make 3   Make 1

Figure 11

16. Repeat steps 8–12 with dark G, H and I strips to complete two each dark White Birch and dark Reverse White Birch blocks as shown in Figure 12.

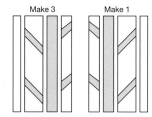

Make 2   Reverse Make 2

Figure 12

Completing the Quilt

1. Join one each light and dark blocks with two medium blocks to make the top row referring to Figure 13; press seams in one direction.

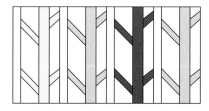

Figure 13

2. Join one each light reverse and medium reverse blocks and two dark reverse blocks to make the center row referring to Figure 14; press seams in one direction.

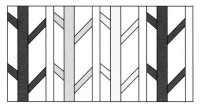

Figure 14

3. Join one each medium and dark block with two light blocks to make the bottom row referring to Figure 15; press seams in one direction.

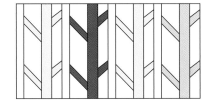

Figure 15

4. Join the rows to complete the quilt center referring to the Placement Diagram for positioning; press seams in one direction.

Adding Appliquéd Birds

1. Trace bird shapes (page 36) onto the paper side of the fusible web, leaving ½" between pieces. Cut out shapes, leaving a margin around each piece.

2. Fuse shapes to the wrong side of fabrics as directed on templates for color; cut out shapes on traced lines. Remove paper backing.

3. Arrange and fuse the bird motifs in place in numerical order on the pieced center referring to the Placement Diagram for positioning. **Note:** *Vary the bird wing placement to individualize each bird.*

4. Using thread to match fabrics and a narrow zigzag stitch, sew around each shape to complete appliqué.

Completing the Quilt

1. Sew K strips to opposite long sides and L strips to the top and bottom of the pieced center; press seams toward K and L strips.

2. Join the M/N strips on short ends to make one long strip; press seams open. Subcut strip into two 60½" M strips and two 46½" N strips.

3. Sew M strips to opposite long sides and N strips to the top and bottom of the pieced center; press seams toward M and N strips.

4. Join the O/P strips on short ends to make one long strip; press seams open. Subcut strip into two 64½" O strips and two 46½" P strips.

5. Fold and press each O and P strip with wrong sides together along the length to make flange strips.

6. Pin a P flange strip to each R strip, matching raw edges, as shown in Figure 16; machine-baste ⅛" from edge to hold in place.

Figure 16

7. Pin and baste an O flange strip to each Q strip as in step 6; add an S rectangle to each end of the basted O/Q strip as shown in Figure 17. Press seams away from S.

8. Sew the P/R strips to the top and bottom, and the O/Q/S strips to opposite long sides of the pieced center to complete the pieced top; press seams toward the M and N strips.

9. Layer, quilt and bind referring to Finishing Your Quilt on page 64. ☐

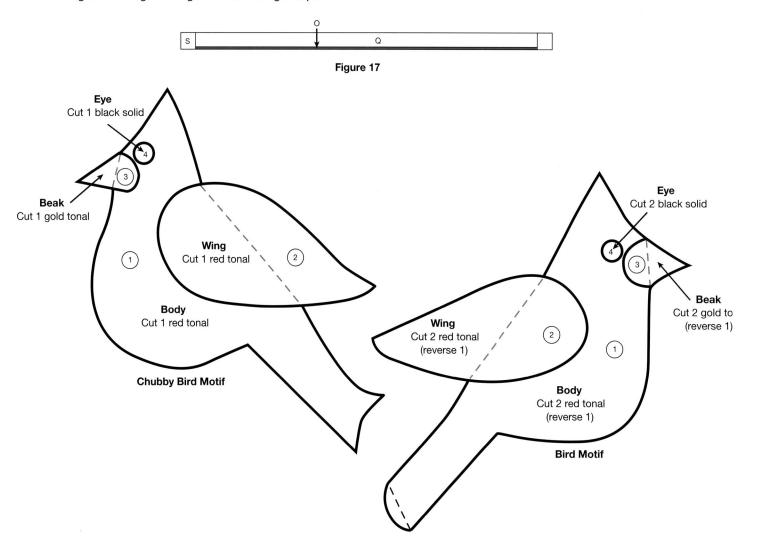

Figure 17

Eye
Cut 1 black solid

Beak
Cut 1 gold tonal

Wing
Cut 1 red tonal

Body
Cut 1 red tonal

Chubby Bird Motif

Eye
Cut 2 black solid

Beak
Cut 2 gold to
(reverse 1)

Wing
Cut 2 red tonal
(reverse 1)

Body
Cut 2 red tonal
(reverse 1)

Bird Motif

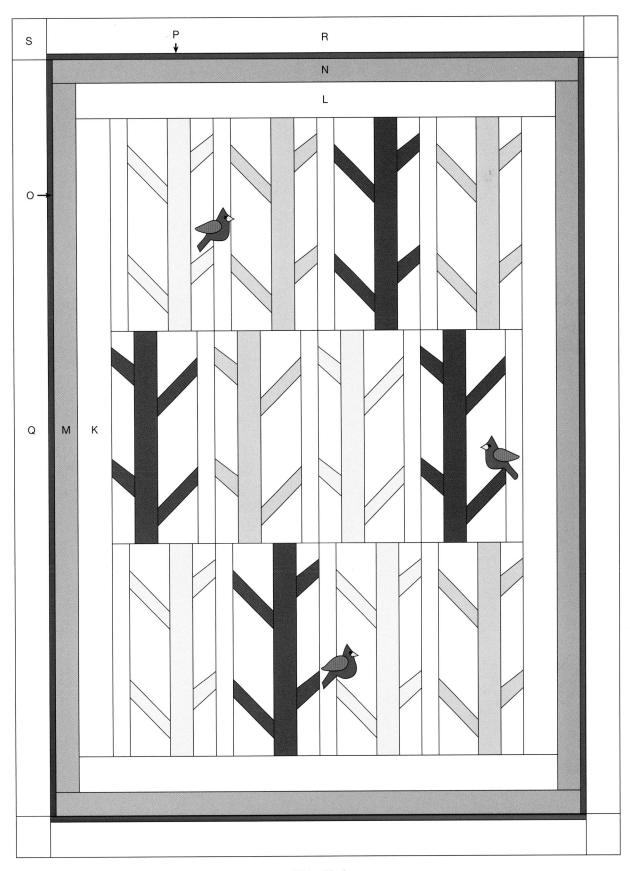

White Birches
Placement Diagram 53" x 71"

My Rose of Sharon

DESIGN BY BEV GETSCHEL, QUILTED BY LEE SPANNER OF ANILEE QUILT CREATIONS

The classic Rose of Sharon gets a new twist and a supersized update. Black and white prints provide the perfect backdrop for the flowers and leaves.

Project Specifications

Skill Level: Intermediate
Quilt Size: 90" x 100"

Materials

- 1 fat quarter gold mottled
- 1 fat quarter each 18 assorted red tonals, mottleds and batiks
- 1 fat quarter each 9 assorted green tonals, mottleds and batiks
- ¾ yard green tonal
- 1¼ yards each 10 assorted white-with-black prints
- 2⅞ yards black solid
- Backing 98" x 108"
- Batting 98" x 108"
- All-purpose thread to match fabrics
- Quilting thread
- Clear nylon monofilament
- 7½ yards black jumbo rickrack
- ½" bias tape maker
- Water-soluble fabric glue stick
- Basic sewing tools and supplies

Cutting

1. From the 10 assorted white-with-black prints, cut a total of 20 (10½" by fabric width) strips. Subcut into 32 (10½") A squares, 67 (5½" x 10½") B rectangles and one 5½" C square.

2. From the black solid, cut seven 3" by fabric width D/E strips and nine 5½" by fabric width F strips.

3. Cut 10 (2¼" by fabric width) strips from the black solid for binding.

Completing the Pieced Background

1. Join two B rectangles along the 10½" sides to make a B unit; press seam to one side. Repeat to make 26 B units.

2. Select one B rectangle, two B units and three A squares; join to make row 1 as shown in Figure 1; press seams toward A squares.

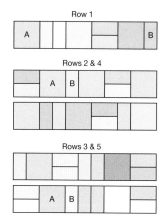

Figure 1

3. Repeat step 2, rearranging the pieces/units to make one each row 2 and row 4.

4. Select one B rectangle, two A squares and three B units; join to make row 3, again referring to Figure 1; press seams toward A squares.

5. Repeat step 4, rearranging the pieces/units to make row 5.

6. Sew a C square to one end of a B rectangle; press seam toward C. Sew a B rectangle to A; press seam toward A. Sew the B-C unit to the A-B unit to make an A-B-C unit as shown in Figure 2; press seam toward the B-C unit.

Figure 2

7. Sew a B rectangle to the seamed edge of a B unit to make a B-B unit, again referring to Figure 2; press seam toward B. Repeat to make two B-B units.

8. Sew a B rectangle to one side of A to make an A-B unit; press seam toward A. Repeat to make two A-B units.

9. Join the A-B-C unit with the A-B and B-B units to make row 6 as shown in Figure 3. Press seams in one direction.

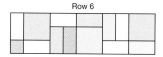

Figure 3

10. Join the rows in numerical order to complete the pieced center; press seams in one direction.

11. Join the D/E strips on short ends to make one long strip; press seams open. Subcut strip into two 65½" D strips and two 60½" E strips.

12. Sew the D strips to opposite long sides and E strips to the top and bottom of the pieced center; press seams toward D and E strips.

13. Join three A squares and four B units to make a side strip referring to Figure 4; press seams toward A squares. Repeat to make two side strips.

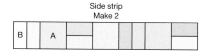

Figure 4

14. Sew a side strip to opposite long sides of the pieced center, turning strips to alternate positioning of pieces referring to the Placement Diagram; press seams toward D strips.

15. Join two B rectangles with two B units and five A squares to make the top strip referring to Figure 5; press seams toward A squares.

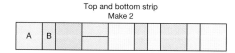

Figure 5

16. Repeat to make the bottom strip, again referring to Figure 5.

17. Sew the top strip to the top and bottom strip to the bottom of the pieced center referring to the Placement Diagram; press seams toward E strips.

18. Join the F strips on short ends to make one long strip; press seams open. Subcut strip into four 90½" F strips.

19. Sew F strips to opposite sides and to the top and bottom of the pieced center; press seams toward F strips.

20. Cut two each identical 61" and 67" lengths black jumbo rickrack. Center a long strip at the seam between the D strips and the pieced center; use water-soluble fabric glue stick to glue-baste in place. Repeat with the 61" lengths on the top and bottom. Turn under edges at corners where the pieces meet; trim excess. Machine-stitch the rickrack in place down the center to secure. **Note:** *If possible, try to make all corners look the same. Cutting identical strips and centering the lengths should help accomplish this.*

Completing the Quilt

1. Prepare templates for appliqué pieces using patterns given (pages 41, 43 and 44); cut as directed on each piece, adding a ¼" seam allowance all around when cutting for appliqué.

2. Turn under edges of each appliqué piece; glue-baste in place using water-soluble fabric glue stick.

3. Using a ½" bias tape maker prepare 300" green mottled bias for stems referring to the manufacturer's instructions.

4. Beginning in the middle of the quilt top, place the eight large petals with ends meeting in the center as shown in Figure 6; using water-soluble fabric glue stick, glue-baste to hold in place.

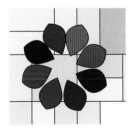

Figure 6

Figure 7

5. Place four matching small petals on the large petals, centering small petal between the large petals as shown in Figure 7; glue-baste in place using water-soluble fabric glue stick.

6. Tuck one end of the stem strip under two large flower petals as shown in Figure 8; hand-stitch that end in place.

Figure 8

7. Center four matching small petals on a pieced side border with the inside petal ¼" from seam between D and the side border strip as shown in Figure 9 on page; glue-baste in place using water-soluble fabric glue stick.

Figure 9

8. Arrange the stem strip from the center flower to the side flower, making an arch, referring to Figure 10; trim at end, leaving an extra inch to tuck under a petal, again referring to Figure 10. Machine-stitch the stem strip in place along both edges using clear nylon monofilament and a blind hemstitch.

Figure 10

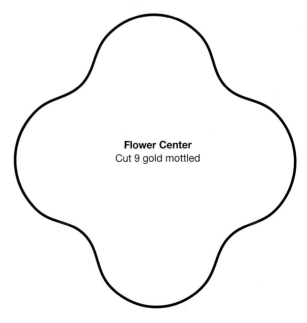

Flower Center
Cut 9 gold mottled

My Rose of Sharon
Placement Diagram 90" x 100"

9. Repeat steps 6–8 to place the first round of four petals on the three remaining pieced borders and one set of four petals in each corner of the quilt center, referring to the Placement Diagram for positioning, tucking stem pieces under the large center petals and curving the stem to the outer flowers before machine stitching the stems in place.

10. Machine-stitch the large and small flower petals of the center flower in place using clear nylon monofilament and a blind hemstitch. Referring to the Placement Diagram, place four more coordinating small petals on top of the stitched center large and small flower petals and machine-stitch in place.

11. For the remaining flowers, machine-stitch each set of four petals in place. Glue-baste four coordinating small petals over the stitched petals referring to the Placement Diagram for positioning; machine-stitch in place.

12. Center and machine-stitch a flower center on each flower motif.

13. Position the leaf shapes on the stems referring to the Placement Diagram for positioning; machine-stitch in place to finish the quilt top.

14. Layer, quilt and bind referring to Finishing Your Quilt on page 64. ❑

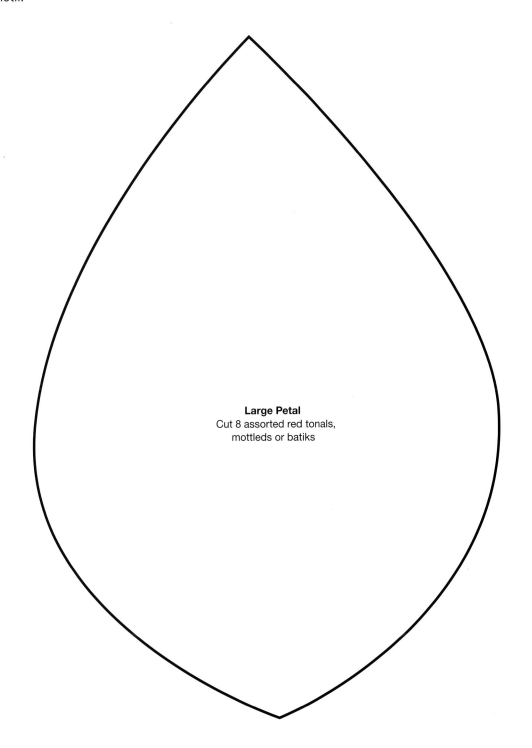

Large Petal
Cut 8 assorted red tonals,
mottleds or batiks

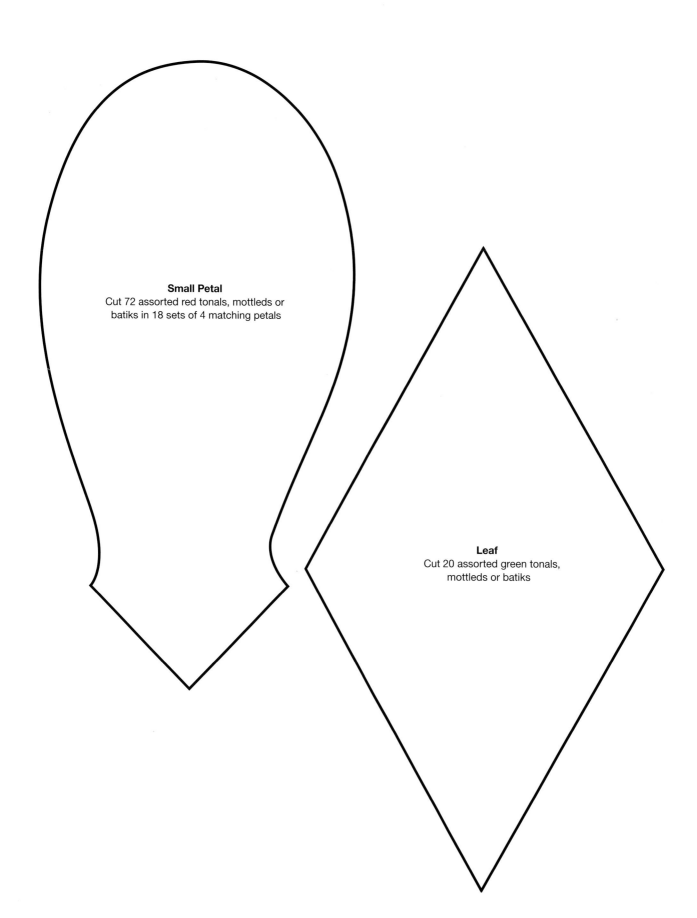

Small Petal
Cut 72 assorted red tonals, mottleds or
batiks in 18 sets of 4 matching petals

Leaf
Cut 20 assorted green tonals,
mottleds or batiks

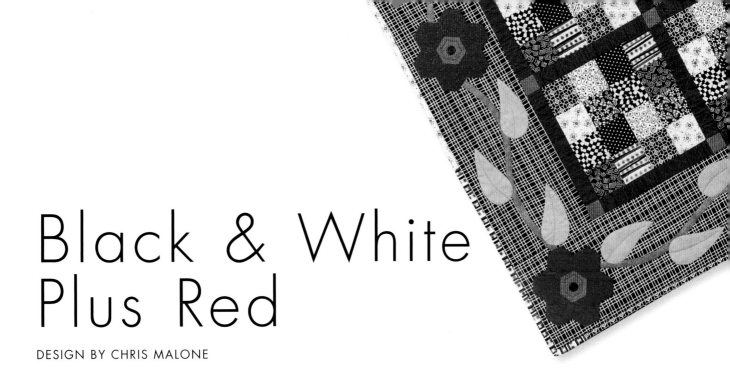

Black & White Plus Red

DESIGN BY CHRIS MALONE

Change the colors of the English paper-pieced flowers and 16-patch blocks to fit your special occasion.

Project Specifications

Skill Level: Intermediate
Quilt Size: 40" x 40"
Block Size: 8" x 8"
Number of Blocks: 9

Materials

- 1 fat quarter orange tonal
- 1 fat quarter red tonal stripe
- 1 fat quarter dark green tonal
- 1 fat quarter lime green tonal
- 2 fat quarters red tonals
- 4 fat quarters black-with-white prints (black)
- 4 fat quarters white-with-black prints (white)
- ⅞ yard black-and-white plaid
- Batting 48" x 48"
- Backing 48" x 48"
- All-purpose thread to match fabrics
- Quilting thread
- 8 (½") black buttons
- 56 precut 1" hexagon paper shapes (optional) or regular-weight white paper
- Water-soluble marker
- Basic sewing tools and supplies

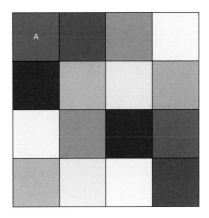

16-Patch
8" x 8" Block
Make 9

Cutting

1. Cut three 2½" x 21" strips from each of the black and white print fat quarters; subcut strips into 18 (2½") A squares each fabric for a total of 144 squares.

2. Cut nine 2¼" x 21" strips total black and white print fat quarters for binding.

3. Cut two 8½" x 21" strips red tonal stripe; subcut strips into 24 (1½") B strips.

4. Cut two 1½" x 21" strips orange tonal; subcut strips into 16 (1½") C squares.

5. Cut two 6½" x 28½" D strips and two 6½" x 40½" E strips black-and-white plaid.

6. Cut eight 1¼" x 15" bias vine strips dark green tonal.

Completing the Blocks

1. Arrange 16 A squares (two of each print) in four rows of four squares each.

2. Join the squares as arranged to make rows; press seams in adjacent rows in opposite directions.

3. Join the rows to complete one 16-Patch block; press seams in one direction.

4. Repeat steps 1–3 to complete nine 16-Patch blocks.

Completing the Top

1. Arrange the blocks in three rows of three blocks; join three blocks from one row with four B strips to make a block row as shown in Figure 1; press seams toward B strips. Repeat to make three block rows.

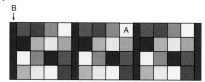

Figure 1

2. Join three B strips with four C squares to make a sashing row as shown in Figure 2; press seams toward B strips. Repeat to make four sashing rows.

Figure 2

3. Join the block rows with the sashing rows to complete the pieced center; press seams toward sashing rows.

4. Sew a D strip to opposite sides and E strips to the top and bottom of the pieced center; press seams toward D and E strips to complete the pieced top.

English Paper Piecing the Flowers

1. To make the English paper-pieced flowers, copy the hexagon pattern given (page 49) onto white paper 56 times if not using precut shapes; carefully cut out each shape.

2. Pin a paper hexagon to the wrong side of one of the red tonals; cut the fabric ¼" larger than the paper piece all around as shown in Figure 3. Repeat to cut 24 hexagons from each of the two red tonals and eight from the orange tonal.

3. To prepare each hexagon for stitching, fold the ¼" seam allowance over the paper shape at precisely

Figure 3

the paper edge; finger-press and hand-baste in place through the fabric and paper using large stitches as shown in Figure 4. To fold corners, continue to fold over the fabric, but include the folded-over seam allowance from the previous side as shown in Figure 5.

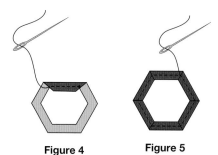

Figure 4   **Figure 5**

4. Secure basting at the end with a small backstitch; clip thread, leaving a ¼" tail. Repeat to prepare all hexagon shapes for the flowers.

5. To hand-stitch one flower, use six matching red hexagons for the petals and one orange for the center. Place one each orange and red hexagon pieces right sides together, and using a knotted single-strand matching thread, insert the needle at one corner under the seam allowance and out the tip; make small whipstitches to overcast the pieces together, just catching the edges of the fabric and only barely missing

the enclosed paper edge. When you have completed the edge, take a second stitch into the corner to secure, and then open the patches flat as shown in Figure 6.

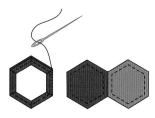

Figure 6

6. Place the second red hexagon on top of the first red hexagon with right sides together; whipstitch the edges from the orange center to the outer edge as in step 5. Tie off the thread and clip. Now fold the patches so the second red hexagon is right sides together with the orange center and hand-sew the edges together. Continue around, adding the red petals until the flower is complete as shown in Figure 7; press.

Figure 7

7. Remove the basting stitches; carefully remove the paper pieces.

8. Repeat steps 5–7 to make a total of eight flowers—four from each red tonal.

Applying Appliqué

1. To make vines, fold each dark green bias vine strip in half along length with wrong sides together; stitch a scant ¼" seam along the raw edges. Trim seam to ⅛" and fold the strip so the seam is open and centered down the length of the vine as shown in Figure 8.

Figure 8

2. Using the pattern given and a water-soluble marker, trace 12 leaf shapes and 12 reversed leaf shapes onto the right side of the lime green tonal; cut out shapes, leaving a ⅛"–¼" seam to turn under all around.

3. Turn under edges of each leaf shape along the marked lines, finger-press, and then hand-baste to hold in place.

4. Place a matching flower at each corner and the remaining four flowers centered on each border strip; hand-baste to hold in place.

5. Arrange and pin a vine in a gentle curving line between the flowers, tucking the vine ends at least ¼" under the edge of the flowers; trim any excess.

6. Arrange and pin three leaves on each vine, referring to the Placement Diagram for positioning; hand-stitch flowers, vine and leaf shapes in place using thread to match fabrics to complete the pieced top.

Completing the Quilt

1. Refer to Finishing Your Quilt on page 64 to layer, quilt and bind your quilt.

2. Sew a black button in the center of each hexagon flower to finish. ☐

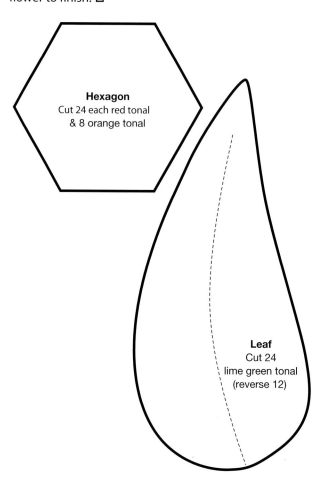

Hexagon
Cut 24 each red tonal
& 8 orange tonal

Leaf
Cut 24
lime green tonal
(reverse 12)

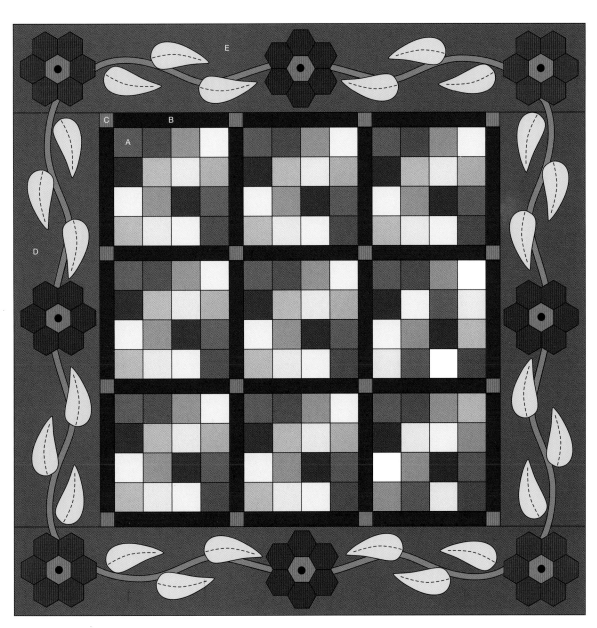

Black & White Plus Red
Placement Diagram 40" x 40"

Children's Silhouette

DESIGN BY CAROLYN S. VAGTS

Capture the essence of childhood in a quilt reminiscent of Victorian silhouette portraiture—no sitting still required.

Project Specifications

Skill Level: Beginner
Quilt Size: 41½" x 60"

Project Notes

The panels used to make this quilt take advantage of the black borders between the preprint blocks in the fabric. When cutting, be sure the preprint motif is centered with equal amounts of bordering fabric all around.

Your local quilt shop may not have this panel, or you may prefer another motif. Any 9" x 7½" or 7½"-square panel will work for this design. Using a special focus fabric in place of the panels would also be a great way to use this quilt design.

Materials

- 7 panels each measuring at least 9" x 7½"*
- 8 panels each measuring at least 7½" square*
- ⅝ yard black solid**
- ⅔ yard black with yellow stripe**
- 1¼ yards yellow with black swirl**
- Backing 50" x 68"
- Batting 50" x 68"
- Neutral-color all-purpose thread
- Basic sewing tools and supplies

*If not using panels, substitute 1 yard of large-print fabric.
**Coordinate these yardages with the colors of your panels or substitute print fabric.

Cutting

1. Trim seven panels (A) to 9" x 7½" and eight panels (B) to 7½" square.

2. If substituting large print for panels, cut four 7½" by fabric width strips. Subcut into seven 7½" x 9" A rectangles and eight 7½" B squares.

3. From the black solid, cut eight 1½" by fabric width F strips and two 1½" x 34" G strips.

4. From the black with yellow stripe, cut four 1¼" by fabric width strips. Subcut into 16 (1¼" x 7½") C rectangles.

5. Cut six 2½" by fabric width strips from the black with yellow stripe for binding.

6. From the yellow with black swirl, cut four 3½" by fabric width strips. Subcut into 15 (3½" x 9") D strips.

7. Cut three 1½" by fabric width yellow with black swirl E strips.

8. Cut two 4½" x 34" yellow with black swirl H strips.

9. Cut three 4½" by fabric width yellow with black swirl I strips.

Completing the Quilt

1. Sew a C strip to opposite sides of B; press seams toward C. Repeat to make eight B-C units.

2. Join two A rectangles with three B-C units and five D rectangles to make a vertical side row as shown in Figure 1; press seams toward D rectangles. Repeat to make two side rows.

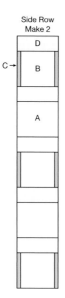

Figure 1

3. Join three A rectangles with two B-C units and five D rectangles to make the center row referring to Figure 2; press seams toward D rectangles.

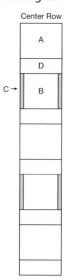

Figure 2

4. Join the E strips on short ends to make one long strip; press seams open. Subcut strip into two 50½" E strips.

5. Join the F strips on short ends to make one long strip; press seams open. Subcut strip into six 50½" F strips.

6. Sew an E strip between two F strips to make an F-E-F strip; press seams toward F strips. Repeat to make two F-E-F strips.

7. Sew an F-E-F strip to opposite long sides of the center row; press seams toward F-E-F strips. Sew a side row to each long side of the bordered center row and add an F strip to each long side referring to the Placement Diagram for positioning.

8. Sew G strips to the top and bottom of the pieced center; press seams toward G strips.

9. Sew an H strip to the top and bottom of the pieced center; press seams toward H strips.

10. Join the I strips on short ends to make one long strip; press seams open. Subcut strip into two 60½" I strips.

11. Sew an I strip to opposite long sides of the pieced center to complete the pieced top.

12. Layer, quilt and bind referring to Finishing Your Quilt on page 64. □

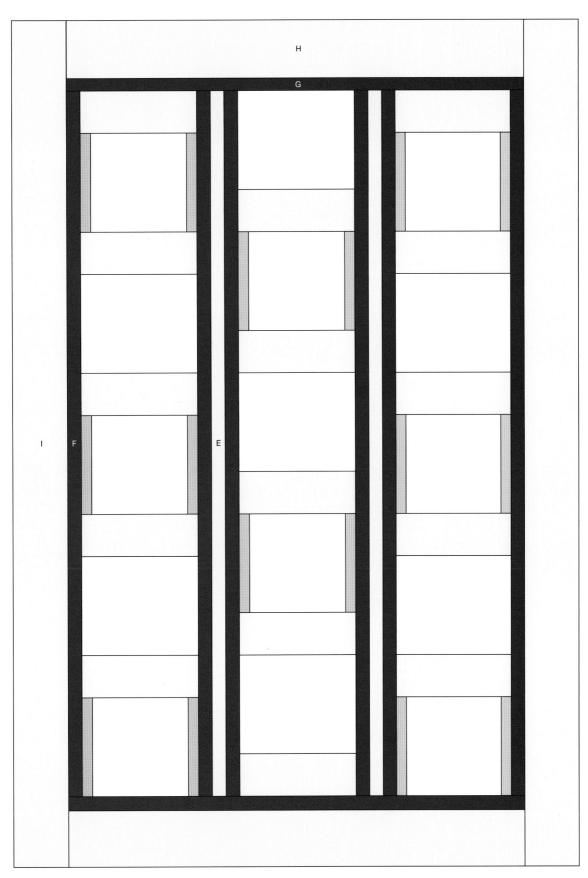

Children's Silhouette
Placement Diagram 41½" x 60"

Starry Lane

DESIGN BY TOBY LISCHKO

Black, gray and white combine with yellow in this striking quilt made with two block patterns.

Project Specifications

Skill Level: Intermediate
Quilt Size: 70" x 94"
Block Size: 12" x 12"
Number of Blocks: 35

Materials

- 5 yellow fat quarters
- 8 white fat quarters
- 9 gray fat quarters
- 12 black fat quarters
- ½ yard yellow tonal
- 1¾ yards black print
- Backing 76" x 100"
- Batting 76" x 100"
- All-purpose thread to match fabrics
- Quilting thread
- Template plastic or poster board
- Basic tools and supplies

Starry Lane A
12" x 12" Block
Make 18

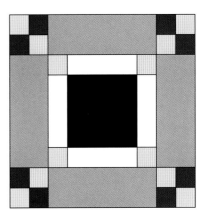

Starry Lane B
12" x 12" Block
Make 17

Cutting

1. Cut six 3¾" x 22" strips yellow; subcut strips into 36 (3¾") B squares.

2. Cut 17 (1¾" x 22") strips yellow. Subcut 11 strips into 136 (1¾") G squares. Set aside six strips.

3. Cut six 3¾" x 22" strips white; subcut strips into 36 (3¾") B squares. Mark one diagonal on the wrong side of each B square.

4. Cut six 1½" x 22" strips white; subcut strips into 72 (1½") C squares.

5. Cut 11 (3" x 22") strips white; subcut strips into 72 (3") D squares.

6. Cut six 5" x 22" strips white; subcut strips into 68 (1¾" x 5") I rectangles.

7. Cut six 6¼" x 22" strips gray; subcut strips into 18 (6¼") squares. Cut each square on both diagonals to make 72 E triangles.

8. Cut 10 (7½" x 22") gray strips; subcut strips into 68 (3" x 7½") J rectangles.

9. Cut six 5½" x 22" strips black; subcut strips into 72 (1½" x 5½") A rectangles.

10. Prepare templates F and FR (page 53) following instructions on patterns. Cut 21 (4⅜" x 22") strips black; subcut strips into 144 (3" x 4⅜") rectangles. Use templates to cut 72 each F and FR pieces from the 3" x 4⅜" rectangles.

11. Cut 12 (1¾" x 22") strips black. Subcut six strips into 68 (1¾") G squares. Set aside six strips.

12. Cut three 5" by fabric width black strips. Subcut 17 (5") H squares.

13. Cut one 3" by fabric width strip black; subcut strip into eight 3" M squares.

14. Cut one 1¾" by fabric width strip each yellow tonal (K) and black print (L).

15. Cut seven 1¾" by fabric width strips yellow tonal; join strips on short ends to make one long strip. Subcut strip into two 84½" N and two 60½" P strips.

16. Cut seven 4¼" by fabric width strips black print; join strips on short ends to make one long strip. Subcut strip into two 84½" O and two 60½" Q strips.

17. Cut nine 2¼" by fabric width strips black print for binding.

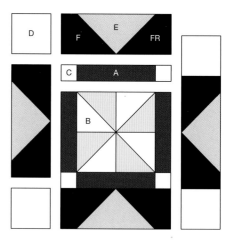

Starry Lane A
Piecing Diagram

Completing the Starry Lane A Blocks

1. Place a white and yellow B square right sides together and stitch ¼" on either side of the diagonal marked on the white B. Cut apart on the marked line. Press seam toward yellow.

2. Repeat with another pair of yellow and white B squares to make four yellow and white half-square B units.

3. Refer to the piecing diagram and sew the units together to make a pieced center.

4. Stitch an A rectangle to two opposite sides of the pieced center. Press seams toward A.

5. Sew a C square to each end of two A rectangles to make two C/A strips.

6. Sew the C/A strips to the remaining sides of the pieced center.

7. Sew F and FR pieces to the short sides of the E triangle, referring to the piecing diagram, to make a side unit. Repeat to make four side units.

8. Sew a side unit to opposite sides of the pieced center. Press seams toward the pieced center.

9. Sew D to opposite ends of the remaining side units, referring to the piecing diagram. Press seams toward D.

10. Sew the D/side units to the remaining sides of the pieced center. Press seams toward the side units.

11. Repeat steps 1–10 to complete 18 Starry Lane A blocks.

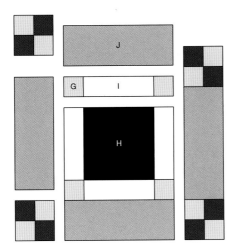

Starry Lane B
Piecing Diagram

Completing the Starry Lane B Blocks

1. Referring to the piecing diagram, sew an I strip to opposite sides of an H square.

2. Sew a G square to either end of an I strip. Repeat to make two I/G strips.

3. Sew the I/G strips to the remaining sides of the H square to complete the pieced center.

4. Sew a yellow strip, set aside in step 2 of Cutting instructions, to a black strip, set aside in step 11 of Cutting instructions, along length. Press seam toward black strip. Repeat to make six strip sets.

5. Subcut the strip sets into 1¾" x 2½" rectangles. Referring to the piecing diagram, sew two rectangles together to make a corner unit. Repeat to make four corner units.

6. Sew J to opposite sides of the pieced center referring to the piecing diagram.

7. Sew a corner unit to each end of one J strip. Repeat to make two J/corner unit strips.

8. Sew the J/corner unit strips to remaining sides of the pieced center to complete one Starry Lane B block.

9. Repeat steps 1–8 to make 17 Starry Lane B blocks.

Completing the Quilt

1. Join three A blocks with two B blocks to make row A referring to Figure 1; repeat for four rows. Press seams toward B blocks.

2. Join three B blocks with two A blocks to make row B, again referring to Figure 1; repeat for three rows. Press seams toward B blocks.

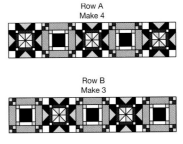

Row A
Make 4

Row B
Make 3

Figure 1

3. Join the rows referring to the Placement Diagram for positioning of rows; press seams in one direction.

4. Sew an N strip to an O strip with right sides together along the length; press seams toward O. Repeat to make two N/O strips.

5. Sew an N/O strip to opposite long sides of the pieced center; press seams toward N/O.

6. Sew a P strip to a Q strip with right sides together along the length; press seams toward Q. Repeat to make two P/Q strips. Set aside.

7. Sew a K strip to an L strip with right sides together along length; press seams toward L. Subcut strip set into 16 (1¾" x 3") K/L segments. Sew two K/L segments together to make a K/L unit; repeat to make eight units.

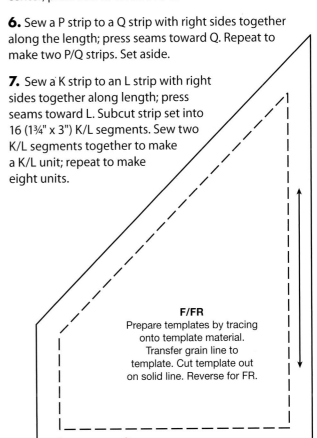

F/FR
Prepare templates by tracing onto template material. Transfer grain line to template. Cut template out on solid line. Reverse for FR.

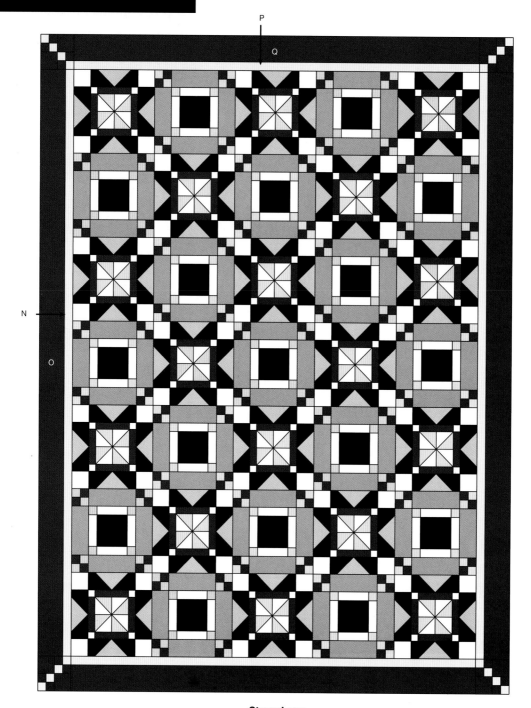

Starry Lane
Placement Diagram 70" x 94"

8. Join one K/L unit with one M square to make a row as shown in Figure 2; press seams toward M. Make two rows and sew together, again referring to Figure 2 to make a corner unit. Repeat to make four corner units.

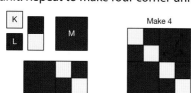

Figure 2

9. Sew a corner unit to each end of a P/Q strip. Repeat to make two P/Q strip sets.

10. Sew a P/Q strip set to the top and bottom of the quilt to finish the quilt top. Press seams toward the P/Q strip sets.

11. Layer, quilt and bind referring to Finishing Your Quilt on page 64. ☐

In the Pink

DESIGN BY SUSAN MAYER

Gather all of your hot pink, eye-catching prints—adding black and white always creates a bit of drama.

Project Specifications

Skill Level: Confident Beginner
Quilt Size: 53" x 63"
Block Size: 10" x 10"
Number of Blocks: 20

Project Notes

The Courthouse Steps block is a variation of the Log Cabin block. The strips are added to opposite sides of the block center instead of in rounds around the block center. In this quilt, adjacent blocks blend into one another with careful planning and placement of strips and colors. Random piecing and color placement will not yield the Japanese lantern shapes so prominent in this Courthouse Steps design. Figure 1 illustrates how the first block in row 1 flows into the second block in row 1 and the first block in row 2. No two blocks are alike, so treat this quilt like a puzzle as you stitch the blocks together.

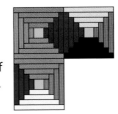

Figure 1

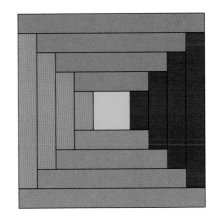

Courthouse Steps
10" x 10" Block

Materials

- ⅛ yard pink print
- ⅛ yard each 20 assorted black fabrics
- ⅛ yard each 20 assorted pink fabrics
- ¼ yard green solid
- ¼ yard black polka dot
- ⅔ yard large pink floral
- 1 yard black circle print
- Backing 61" x 71"
- Batting 61" x 71"
- Neutral-color all-purpose thread
- Quilting thread
- Basic sewing tools and supplies

Cutting

Note: *Fabric measurements are based on a 43" usable fabric width.*

1. Cut two 1½" x 40½" B strips from the pink print.

2. Cut two 1½" by fabric width strips from each of the 20 assorted black fabrics. Use for pieces 3, 4, 7, 8 11, 12, 15 and 16 as instructed in steps 1–4 of Completing the Blocks & Rows.

3. From each of the 20 assorted pink fabrics, cut two 1½" by fabric width strips. Use for pieces 1, 2, 5, 6, 9, 10, 13 and 14 as instructed in steps 1–4 of Completing the Blocks & Rows.

4. From the green solid, cut two 2½" by fabric width strips. Subcut into 20 (2½") A squares.

5. From the black polka dot, cut three 1½" by fabric width C strips.

6. From the large pink floral, cut three 6" by fabric width E side strips.

7. From the black circle print, cut two 6" x 42½" D strips.

8. Cut six 2¼" by fabric width strips from the black circle print for binding.

Completing the Blocks & Rows

1. Select one A square and four different-color 1½"-wide strips.

2. Referring to Figure 2 for strip numbers, sew the A square to strip 1 as shown in Figure 3; trim the strip even with A and press open with seam toward strip 1 as shown in Figure 4.

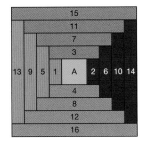

Figure 2

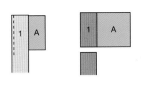

Figure 3   **Figure 4**

3. Repeat step 2 on the opposite side of A with strip 2 referring to Figure 5.

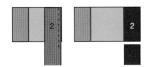

Figure 5

4. Continue adding strips to opposite sides of A in numerical order until you have four strips on each side of A as shown in Figure 6.

Figure 6

5. Repeat steps 1–4 using one A square, one matching fabric from prior block and three different fabrics to complete four blocks for the first row, stitching one block at a time and arranging the blocks in rows as stitched, with matching fabric placed next to each other.

6. When four blocks are complete for one row, join to make the row as shown in Figure 7 to avoid confusion later; press seams in one direction.

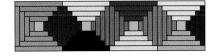

Figure 7

7. Continue making four blocks for the second row, matching fabric colors from block to block and row to row until you have completed the row referring to Figure 8. Press seams in the opposite direction from row 1; join the two rows.

Figure 8

8. Continue in this manner until you have completed the pieced center with five rows of four blocks each.

Completing the Quilt

1. Sew a B strip to the top and bottom of the quilt center; press seams toward B strips.

2. Join the C strips on short ends to make one long strip; press seams open. Subcut strip into two 52½" C strips. Sew a C strip to opposite long sides of the quilt center; press seams toward C strips.

3. Sew the D strips to the top and bottom of the quilt center; press seams toward D strips.

4. Join the E strips on short ends to make one long strip; press seams open. Subcut strip into two 63½" E strips. Sew an E strip to opposite long sides of the quilt center; press seams toward E strips to complete the pieced top.

5. Layer, quilt and bind referring to Finishing Your Quilt on page 64. ☐

In the Pink
Placement Diagram 53" x 63"

Finishing Your Quilt

Step 1. Sandwich the batting between the completed top and prepared backing; pin or baste layers together to hold. **Note:** *If using basting spray to hold layers together, refer to instructions on the product container for use.*

Step 2. Quilt as desired by hand or machine; remove pins or basting. Trim excess backing and batting even with quilt top.

Step 3. Join binding strips on short ends to make one long strip. Fold the strip in half along length with wrong sides together; press.

Step 4. Sew binding to quilt edges, mitering corners and overlapping ends. Fold binding to the back side and stitch in place to finish.

Metric Conversion Charts

Metric Conversions

Canada/U.S. Measurement		Multiplied by		Metric Measurement
yards	x	.9144	=	metres (m)
yards	x	91.44	=	centimetres (cm)
inches	x	2.54	=	centimetres (cm)
inches	x	25.40	=	millimetres (mm)
inches	x	.0254	=	metres (m)

Canada/U.S. Measurement		Multiplied by		Metric Measurement
centimetres	x	.3937	=	inches
metres	x	1.0936	=	yards

Standard Equivalents

Canada/U.S. Measurement				Metric Measurement
⅛ inch	=	3.20 mm	=	0.32 cm
¼ inch	=	6.35 mm	=	0.635 cm
⅜ inch	=	9.50 mm	=	0.95 cm
½ inch	=	12.70 mm	=	1.27 cm
⅝ inch	=	15.90 mm	=	1.59 cm
¾ inch	=	19.10 mm	=	1.91 cm
⅞ inch	=	22.20 mm	=	2.22 cm
1 inch	=	25.40 mm	=	2.54 cm
⅛ yard	=	11.43 cm	=	0.11 m
¼ yard	=	22.86 cm	=	0.23 m
⅜ yard	=	34.29 cm	=	0.34 m
½ yard	=	45.72 cm	=	0.46 m
⅝ yard	=	57.15 cm	=	0.57 m
¾ yard	=	68.58 cm	=	0.69 m
⅞ yard	=	80.00 cm	=	0.80 m
1 yard	=	91.44 cm	=	0.91 m
1⅛ yards	=	102.87 cm	=	1.03 m
1¼ yards	=	114.30 cm	=	1.14 m

Canada/U.S. Measurement				Metric Measurement
1⅜ yards	=	125.73 cm	=	1.26 m
1½ yards	=	137.16 cm	=	1.37 m
1⅝ yards	=	148.59 cm	=	1.49 m
1¾ yards	=	160.02 cm	=	1.60 m
1⅞ yards	=	171.44 cm	=	1.71 m
2 yards	=	182.88 cm	=	1.83 m
2⅛ yards	=	194.31 cm	=	1.94 m
2¼ yards	=	205.74 cm	=	2.06 m
2⅜ yards	=	217.17 cm	=	2.17 m
2½ yards	=	228.60 cm	=	2.29 m
2⅝ yards	=	240.03 cm	=	2.40 m
2¾ yards	=	251.46 cm	=	2.51 m
2⅞ yards	=	262.88 cm	=	2.63 m
3 yards	=	274.32 cm	=	2.74 m
3⅛ yards	=	285.75 cm	=	2.86 m
3¼ yards	=	297.18 cm	=	2.97 m
3⅜ yards	=	308.61 cm	=	3.09 m
3½ yards	=	320.04 cm	=	3.20 m
3⅝ yards	=	331.47 cm	=	3.31 m
3¾ yards	=	342.90 cm	=	3.43 m
3⅞ yards	=	354.32 cm	=	3.54 m
4 yards	=	365.76 cm	=	3.66 m
4⅛ yards	=	377.19 cm	=	3.77 m
4¼ yards	=	388.62 cm	=	3.89 m
4⅜ yards	=	400.05 cm	=	4.00 m
4½ yards	=	411.48 cm	=	4.11 m
4⅝ yards	=	422.91 cm	=	4.23 m
4¾ yards	=	434.34 cm	=	4.34 m
4⅞ yards	=	445.76 cm	=	4.46 m
5 yards	=	457.20 cm	=	4.57 m